Explore Latin
Avēs

Explore Latin
Series Information

The *Explore Latin* series provides novice Latin learners with short, nonfiction texts on a range of subjects related to the ancient world. Each reader in the series uses approximately one-hundred unique Latin words or fewer to describe a topic, employing repetition of key vocabulary and extensive visual support to make information more readily comprehensible. Image labels and other aids further clarify vocabulary and concepts. An introduction explains how to use the book, a full Latin-to-English glossary lists all inflected forms in the text alongside standard dictionary entries, and an index indicates vocabulary used to label images.

Ideal for independent reading or to introduce cultural concepts in the classroom, each volume in the *Explore Latin* series can function both as a stand-alone text and as a pre-reader that prepares learners to transition to the more complex Latin of the *Encounter Latin* novella series. For more information and updates, check our website: www.BOLCHAZY.com.

Explore Latin
Avēs

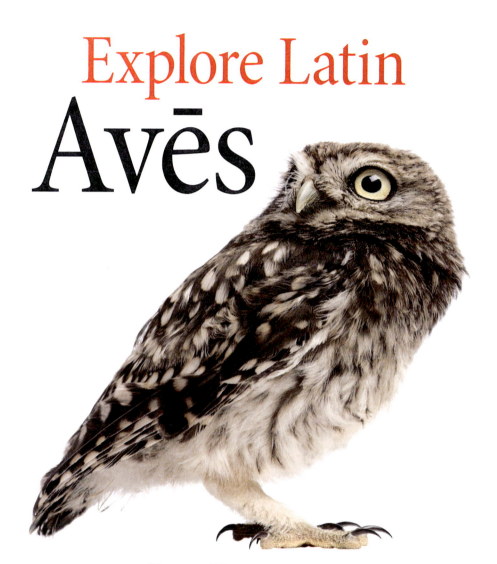

EMMA VANDERPOOL

Bolchazy-Carducci Publishers, Inc.
Wauconda, Illinois USA

Editor: Amelia Wallace
Design & Layout: Adam Phillip Velez

Explore Latin: Avēs

Emma Vanderpool

© 2020 Bolchazy-Carducci Publishers, Inc.
All rights reserved.

Bolchazy-Carducci Publishers, Inc.
1000 Brown Street
Wauconda, Illinois 60084
www.bolchazy.com

Printed in the United States of America
2020
by Publishers' Graphics

ISBN 978-0-86516-874-9

Library of Congress Control Number: 2020944640

Contents

Preface	vii
Introduction: *How to Use This Book*	1
In Caelō	5
Aquilae	11
Vulturēs	19
Corvī	29
Cornīcēs	33
Būbōnēs	39
Pāvōnēs	45
Ānserēs	51
Pullī	55
Latin-to-English Glossary	61
Index of Labeled Vocabulary	67
Image Credits	69

Preface

The field of Latin teaching is undergoing a shift toward supplying students with materials that are both comprehensible and compelling. Teachers are looking for materials that meet students where they are linguistically, while remaining centered on culture and history. By introducing content related to Roman augury and religion to students early on in their Latin career, I hope that they can gain important insight into Roman daily life while remaining in the target language. There is a need and a want for such texts, and so I have been delighted to embark upon this journey with Bolchazy-Carducci Publishers.

    I am enormously grateful to Amelia Wallace at Bolchazy-Carducci for her vision and for meticulously reading through the manuscript and working with me through the image-selection process. Allyson Spencer-Bunch and Chris Mural graciously took the time to pilot the text with their students, even as external circumstances required a sudden transition to online classes. Gregory P. Stringer gave critical feedback and edits on the text itself; any errors that remain are my own.

    I dedicate this book to Dr. Teresa Ramsby and the legions of *collegae* from the University of Massachusetts Amherst MAT program, who have inspired and encouraged me to continually innovate.

Emma Vanderpool
Springfield, MA

Introduction

How to Use This Book

The readers in the *Explore Latin* series are intended to introduce novice Latin learners to an array of ancient topics, using limited vocabulary and abundant textual supports. In ninety unique Latin words, *Explore Latin: Avēs* provides a basic, foundational vocabulary centered around Roman understandings of birds, drawing on terminology from Cicero's writings on augury in *De Divinatione*. This immersive exploration of birds—and their connection to augury (bird divination) and Roman religion more generally—offers readers a unique window into Roman culture. Vivid, full-color images help learners visualize the Latin that they encounter, allowing them to more easily make meaning of the text, while reducing the need to use English as an intermediary.

A number of features helps make this *Explore Latin* book more readily comprehensible, whether it is being used as independent reading material or as a classroom text. First, a **vocabulary tree** appears at the end of this introduction. This vocabulary tree previews some key terms and establishes a graphic representation of how these words relate to one another. Questions and categories included in the tree can prompt class discussion: can students think of additional words they might place in the tree? It may be fruitful to return to the tree and add to it while reading (or after finishing) the book.

The high-interest images that illustrate the text of *Explore Latin: Avēs* include both wildlife photography and art from the ancient Mediterranean and beyond. Latin labels indicate important terms;

Introduction

repetition of these words, alongside pictures, can aid language acquisition. For those reading this book as a class, labeled illustrations can be used for picture talks (describing an image and asking questions about what is depicted entirely in Latin). Examining and analyzing artwork and artifacts from ancient Rome can spark discussion about how these products fit within the larger context of Roman culture. All images used in this book are listed in the **image credits** on page 69 so that those who are interested can conduct further research.

A **Latin-to-English glossary** lists all inflected forms that appear in the text, in addition to standard dictionary entries. While not a focus of this book, some short, functional grammar explanations further clarify concepts. An **index of labeled vocabulary** offers another resource for reviewing (or previewing) repeated vocabulary used in this reader.

Vocabulary Tree

Animālia

Avēs

Quālēs?	Quid agunt?	Partēs Avis
magnae	volant	pennae
parvae	ambulant	ālae
ferōcēs	canunt	rōstrum
pulchrae	pugnant et necant	oculī

In Caelō

Avēs in caelō sunt.

Avēs in caelō volant.

Multae nūbēs in caelō sunt.

Multae avēs et multae nūbēs in caelō sunt.

Avēs duās ālās habent.

Avēs ālīs volant.

In ālīs sunt multae pennae.

Avēs duōs oculōs habent.

Avēs oculīs vident.

Avēs ūnum rōstrum habent.

Multae avēs rōstrō pugnant.

penna, pennae, *f.*

Avēs in caelō volant.

Augurēs avēs in caelō spectant.

Augurēs sunt virī quī avēs
  in caelō spectant.

Avēs sunt signa deōrum.

Augurēs signa deōrum intellegunt.

Augurēs lituum portant.

lituus, lituī, *m.*

Aquilae

Iuppiter deus est.

Iuppiter rēx deōrum est.

Aquila est avis magna et ferōx.

Aquilae sunt avēs Iovis, rēgis deōrum.

Iuppiter, Iovis, *m.*

aquila, aquilae, *f.*

Ecce! Mīles Rōmānus est.

Mīlitēs Rōmānī signum portant.

In signō Rōmānō est aquila.

signum, signī, *n.*

Aquila pennās habet.

Pennae fuscae sunt.

Aquilae rōstrum magnum habent.

Ubi aquilae canunt, clangunt: "clang-clang!"

Aquilae vōcem magnam habent.

serpēns, serpentis, *m./f.*

Aquilae avēs ferōcēs sunt.

Hae aquilae cum serpentibus pugnant.

Hostēs necant!

Vulturēs

Ecce! Sunt vultur et aquila.

Hae avēs ferōcēs sunt.

Aquilae sunt magnae, sed vulturēs maiōrēs sunt!

Vulturēs maiōrēs quam aquilae sunt.

Vulturēs ālās ātrās et magnum rōstrum habent.

Sunt multī vulturēs in caelō.

Vulturēs volant tum hūc, tum illūc.

Vulturēs vōcem nōn magnam sed parvam habent.

Ubi vulturēs canunt, pulpant: "pul-pul."

buunt. Denicq; dum
moyses eleuabat man
suas. supabat irl'm.
Cu v remittebat eas
qualescebat amalech.
Sic q omr sci in hoc
figurant. q tanqua
aues pfistentes. puo
niunt ad regna celor
uelut ad qetis portu.
Eseticles aute spuita
lis nature. s; irruent
ao mortalib; opib;
uacantes. excluis sunt
a regno celor. z mor
tui cu mortuis putt.
Vn dur i euugelio.

Sinite mortuos sepeli
re mortuos suos. Ethi
molog'
Conuenient
q dicit phylosoph'
de hac ybide. Auis ybi
nili fluminis. q semet
ipam purgat. figens
rostru suu i anu suu.
aqm fundit. Hec ser
pentium oua uescit z
morticina. z ex eis
q tillimu cibum depor
tat in nidis suis.

de vulpe dolosa.

vulpēs, vulpis, *f.*   vultur, vulturis, *m.*

Vulturēsavēs ferōcēs sunt.
Vulturēs hostēs necant.

Ecce! Vulpēs et vulturēs sunt.
Trēs vulturēs in vulpe sedent.

Corvī

Ecce! Est corvus.

Corvus est magna avis.

Corvus prope deum Apollinem sedet.

Corvus est avis Apollinis.

Deus Apollō vōcem pūrissimam corvō dat.

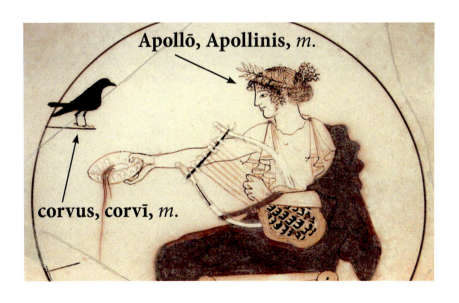

Corvī vōcem pūrissimam habent.
Ubi corvī canunt, dīcunt "crās-crās."

لا يقوى عليه د ينبغي لنا ان نكون على حذر وتأهب لقتالنا فان هن اتينا لقتالنا قابلنا هن وصبرنا لها مواسه فلعل الله ان نظفر بهن ثم قال للخامس مأترى انت فيما قاله اصحابك قال لم يقولوا شيا فانه ينبغي لنا ان له ننصب لقتالهن اليوم ما نجد له الى غير سبيله لهن اقوى علينا منا وقد قيل ان من لم يعرف قدر نفسه ونصبها لقتال عدوه الاقوى فقد اراد هلكها والنفس لها فليس بعاقل من ازدرى عدوه وان كان مهينا ولكنه جى علينا ان نوادعهن فانا ولوكنا اقوى منهن كان ينبغى لنا ان نفعل ذلك حتى نفعد وعلى حاجتنا فان المراة الضعيفة اذا الم يأخذ وجهها بالبين والخد عجبة واراد اخذها بالضرب والهوان لم يستقر عنده ولم تعرطف عليه ولا ارى قتالنا اليوم نات العدو القوى وان كنا بعيدا منا ينبغى ان نغتر بذلك منه
وهذه صورة ملك الغربان يشاور الخمسة خ اسمع

Cornīcēs

Ecce! Sunt cornīcēs!

Cornīcēs sunt parvae avēs.

Multae cornīcēs prope arborem sedent.

Hae avēs similēs sunt.
Pennās ātrās habent.
Rōstrum ātrum habent.

Hae avēs dissimilēs sunt.
Corvī sunt magnī.
Cornīcēs sunt parvae.
Corvī sunt maiōrēs quam cornīcēs.

corvus, corvī, *m.*

cornix, cornīcis, *f.*

Ubi cornīcēs canunt, vōcem pūrissimam nōn habent.

Vōcem raucam habent.

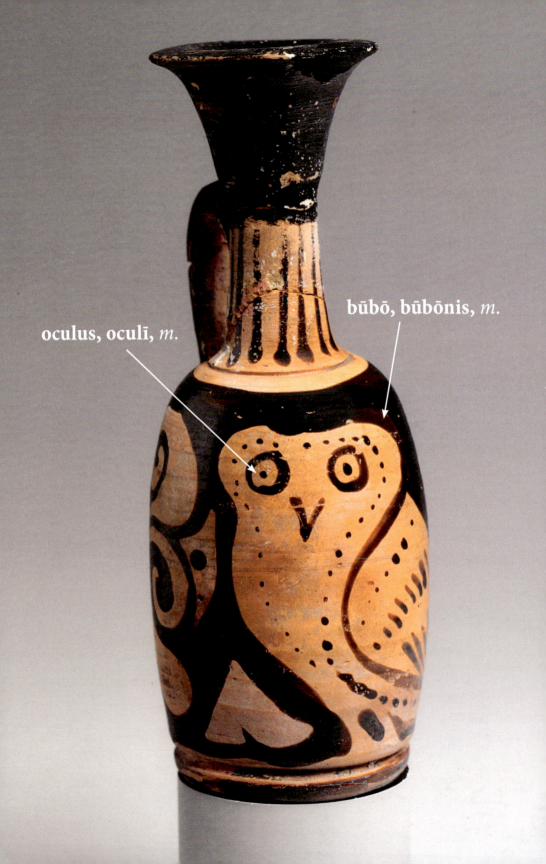

Būbōnēs

Ecce! Est būbō.

Būbōnēs magnae avēs sunt.

Būbōnēs oculōs magnōs habent.

Pennās fuscās et ātrās habent.

In pictūrā est Minerva.

Minerva est dea.

Būbō est avis Minervae.

arma, armōrum, *n.*

Būbōnēs avēs ferōcēs sunt.

Hostēs necant.

In pictūrā būbō est mīles et arma portat!

Ubi būbōnēs canunt, cūcubant: "cū-cū."

Pāvōnēs

Ecce! Est pāvō.

Pennās caeruleās et viridēs habet.

Multae avēs volant.

Pāvōnēs nōn volant sed ambulant.

Pāvōnēs pennās pulchrās habent.

Avēs pulchrae sunt.

Haec est dea Iūnō.

Iūnō est rēgīna deōrum.

Pāvō prope deam sedet.

Pāvō est avis Iūnōnis.

ānser, ānseris, *m./f.*

Ānserēs

Ecce! Est ānser!
Ānser quoque est avis deae Iūnōnis.

Ānserēs avēs ferōcēs sunt.

Magnam vōcem habent:
nōn cūcubant, nōn pulpant,
sed sclingunt!

Ubi Gallī cum mīlitibus Rōmānīs pugnāvērunt, ānserēs magnō clāmōre Rōmam servāvērunt!

Hī ānserēs pennās albās habent.

ānser, ānseris, *m./f.*

penna alba

Pullī

Ecce! Sunt pullī.

Pullī avēs parvae sunt.

Pullī sunt minōrēs quam ānserēs.

Pullī nōn volant, sed ambulant tum hūc, tum illūc.

Pullī pennās albās et fuscās habent.
Pullī parvī pīpiunt: "pī-pī."

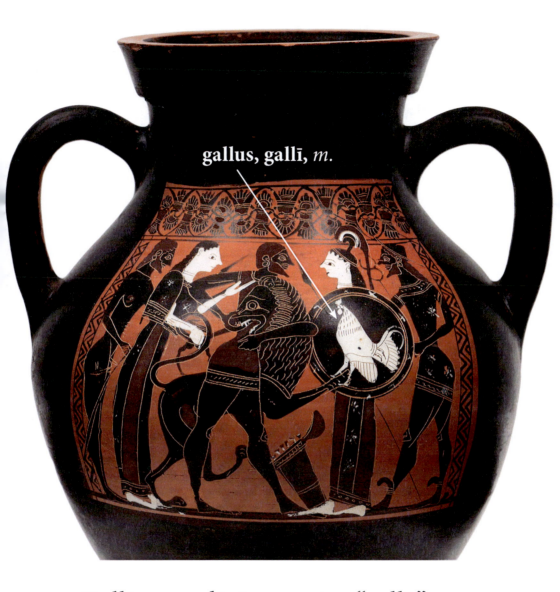

Pullī masculīnī vocantur "gallī."

Gallī sunt avēs ferōcēs.

Hic gallus est ferōcissimus.

Sunt multae avēs.

Sunt avēs magnae.

Sunt avēs parvae.

Augurēs avēs in caelō spectant.

Latin-to-English Glossary

This glossary provides English definitions for all Latin words that appear in this *Explore Latin* reader. Latin terms appear in two formats: (1) as headwords similar to those found in most standard Latin dictionaries and (2) as the inflected words (words with different endings) used throughout the book.

Inflected forms appear under their related headword and include hints about how to understand the form within the context of a Latin sentence. For example, a noun form that can function as the subject of a sentence (the person or thing that *does the action* of a sentence) is labeled *subject*. A noun form that can function as the object of a sentence (the person or thing *affected by the action* of a sentence) is labeled *object*. Special attention is given to how each noun form is functioning within this book. Verb endings in Latin can imply the subject of a sentence; inflected verbs are given with their implied subject. For example, the verb **canunt** is defined as *(they) sing*.

While adjectives can have a variety of endings in Latin, their meanings do not tend to change significantly depending on the ending. Rather, adjective endings often will show which noun the adjective describes. Therefore, separate meanings are not generally given for each adjective form used in the book, although all forms that appear in the book are listed.

Explore Latin: Avēs

List of Abbreviations

(1) = first conjugation
f. = feminine
m. = masculine

n. = neuter
pl. = plural

āla, ālae, *f.,* wing
    ālās, wings (*object*)
    ālīs, with (their) wings
    in ālīs, on (their) wings
albus, -a, -um, white
    alba
    albās
ambulō (1), walk
    ambulant, (they) walk
ānser, ānseris, *m./f.,* goose
    ānser, goose (*subject*)
    ānserēs, geese (*subject*)
Apollō, Apollinis, *m.,* Apollo; god of light, poetry, and music
    Apollinem, Apollo (*object*)
    Apollinis, of Apollo
aquila, aquilae, *f.,* eagle
    aquila, eagle (*subject*)
    aquilae, eagles (*subject*)
arbor, arboris, *f.,* tree
    prope arborem, near the tree
arma, armōrum, *n. pl.,* weapons
    arma, weapons (*object*)

āter, ātra, ātrum, black
    ātra
    ātrās
    ātrum
augur, auguris, *m.,* augur
    augurēs, augurs (*subject*)
avis, avis, *f.,* bird
    avēs, birds (*subject*)
    avis, bird (*subject*)
būbō, būbōnis, *m.,* owl
    būbō, owl (*subject*)
    būbōnēs, owls (*subject*)
caelum, caelī, *n.,* sky, heaven
    in caelō, in the sky
caeruleus, caerulea, caeruleum, blue
    caeruleae
    caeruleās
canō, canere, cecinī, cantum, sing
    canunt, (they) sing
clāmor, clāmōris, *m.,* noise, clamor
    clāmōre, with noise
clangō, clangere, clang, scream
    clangunt, (they) clang, scream

Latin-to-English Glossary

cornix, cornīcis, *f.,* crow
    cornīcēs, crows (*subject*)
corvus, corvī, *m.,* raven
    corvī, ravens (*subject*)
    corvō, to the raven
    corvus, raven (*subject*)
cūcubō (1), hoot
    cūcubant, (they) hoot
cum, with
dō, dare, dedī, datus, give
    dat, (he/she/it) gives
dea, deae, *f.,* goddess
    dea, goddess (*subject*)
    prope deam, near the goddess
deus, deī, *m.,* god
    deōrum, of the gods
    deus, god (*subject*)
    prope deum, near the god
dīcō, dīcere, dīxī, dictum, say, speak, tell
    dīcunt, (they) say
dissimilis, dissimile, dissimilar
    dissimilēs
duo, duae, duo, two
    duās
    duōs
ecce, look!, behold!
est, (he/she/it) is (*see* **sum**)
ferōx, ferōcis, bold, courageous, fierce
    ferōcēs
    ferōcissimus, most bold/boldest, most courageous, most fierce/fiercest
    ferōx
fuscus, -a, -um, brown
    fuscae
    fuscās
Gallī, Gallōrum, *m.,* Gauls, inhabitants of what is modern-day France
    Gallī, Gauls (*subject*)
gallus, gallī, *m.,* rooster
    gallī, roosters (*subject*)
habeō, habēre, habuī, habitum, have, hold
    habent, (they) have
    habet, (he/she/it) has
hic, haec, hoc, this, these
    hae, these
    haec, this
    hī, these
    hic, this
hostis, hostis, *m.,* enemy
    hostēs, enemies (*object*)
hūc, to this place, (to) here, hither
    tum hūc, tum illūc, (then) to this place, then to that place
illūc, to that place, (to) there, thither
    tum hūc, tum illūc, (then) to this place, then to that place

Explore Latin: Avēs

in, in, on
intellegō, intellegere, intellēxī, intellēctum, come to know, understand
    intellegunt, (they) come to know, understand
Iūnō, Iūnōnis, *f.,* Juno, goddess of marriage
    Iūnō, Juno (*subject*)
    Iūnōnis, of Juno
Iuppiter, Iovis, *m.,* Jupiter, god of the sky
    Iovis, of Jupiter
lituus, lituī, *m.,* crooked staff, augur's crook
    lituum, crooked staff, augur's crook (*object*)
magnus, -a, -um, big, great, large
    magna
    magnae
    magnam
    magnī
    magnō
    magnōs
    magnum
maior, maius, bigger, greater, larger
    maiōrēs
masculīnus, -a, -um, male, masculine
    masculīnī

mīles, mīlitis, *m.,* soldier
    cum mīlitibus, with soldiers
    mīles, soldier (*subject*)
    mīlitēs, soldiers (*subject*)
Minerva, -ae, *f.,* Minerva, goddess of wisdom
    Minerva, Minerva (*subject*)
    Minervae, of Minerva
minor, minus, smaller, lesser
    minōrēs
multus, -a, -um, many
    multae
    multī
necō (1), kill
    necant, they kill
nōn, not
nūbēs, nūbis, *f.,* cloud
    nūbēs, clouds (*subject*)
oculus, -ī, *m.,* eye
    oculīs, with eyes
    oculōs, eyes (*object*)
parvus, -a, -um, small
    parvae
    parvās
    parvī
pāvō, pāvōnis, *m.,* peacock
    pāvō, peacock (*subject*)
    pāvōnēs, peacocks (*subject*)
penna, -ae, *f.,* feather
    pennae, feathers (*subject*)
    pennās, feathers (*object*)

Latin-to-English Glossary

pictūra, -ae, *f.*, picture
    in pictūrā, in the picture
pīpiō, pīpīre, peep, chirp
    pīpiunt, (they) peep, chirp
portō (1), carry, bear
    portant, (they) carry, bear
    portat, (he/she/it) carries, bears
prope, near
pugnō (1), fight
    pugnant, (they) fight
    pugnāvērunt, (they) fought
pulcher, pulchra, pulchrum, beautiful, fair, handsome
    pulchrae
    pulchrās
pullus, -ī, *m.*, chicken
    pullī, chickens (*subject*)
pulpō, pulpāre, utter the cry of the vulture, cry
    pulpant, (they) cry
pūrissimus, -a, -um, most pure
    pūrissimam
quam, than
quī, quae, quod, who, which
    quī, who, which (*subject*)
quoque, also

raucus, -a, -um, hoarse
    raucam
rēgīna, -ae, *f.*, queen
    rēgīna, queen (*subject*)
rēx, rēgis, *m.*, king
    rēgis, of the king
    rēx, king (*subject*)
Rōma, -ae, *f.*, Rome
    Rōmam, Rome (*object*)
Rōmānus, -a, -um, Roman
    Rōmānī
    Rōmānō
    Rōmānus
rōstrum, -ī, *n.*, beak
    rōstrō, with (their) beak
    rōstrum, beak (*object*)
sclingō, sclingere, sclingīvī, sclingītum, squawk
    sclingunt, (they) squawk
sed, but
sedeō, sedēre, sēdī, sessum, sit
    sedent, (they) sit
    sedet, (he/she/it) sits
serpēns, serpentibus, *m./f.*, snake
    cum serpentibus, with snakes
servō (1), make safe, save, protect
    servāvērunt, (they) made safe, saved, protected

Explore Latin: Avēs

signum, signī, *n.,* military standard, sign
   in signō, on the military standard
   signa, signs (*subject/object*)
   signum, military standard (*object*)
similis, simile, similar
   similēs
spectō (1), look at, behold, watch
   spectant, (they) look at, behold, watch
sum, esse, fuī, futūrum, be
   est, (he/she/it) is
   sunt, (they) are
sunt, (they) are (*see* **sum**)
trēs, tria, three
   trēs
tum, then
   tum hūc, tum illūc, (then) to this place, then to that place

ubi, when
ūnus, -a, -um, one
   ūnum
videō, vidēre, vīdī, vīsum, see
   vident, (they) see
vir, virī, *m.,* man
   virī, men (*subject*)
viridis, viride, green
   viridēs
vocō (1), call
   vocantur, (they) are called
vox, vōcis, *f.,* voice
   vōcem, voice (*object*)
volō (1), fly
   volant, (they) fly
vulpēs, vulpis, *f.,* fox
   in vulpe, on the fox
   vulpēs, fox (*subject*)
vultur, vulturis, *m.,* vulture
   vultur, vulture (*subject*)
   vulturēs, vultures (*subject*)

Index of Labeled Vocabulary

Below, you will find a listing of the Latin words and phrases used to label images throughout this *Explore Latin* reader. Page numbers designate only the image labels that contain these terms rather than the main text.

āla, ālae, *f.,* 6
    āla ātra, 21
ānser, ānseris, *m./f.,* 50, 53
Apollō, Apollinis, *m.,* 29
aquila, aquilae, *f.,* 11, 13, 18
arbor, arboris, *f.,* 32
arma, armōrum, *n.,* 42
augur, auguris, *m.,* 7
avis, avis, *f.,* 4, 8
būbō, būbōnis, *m.,* 38, 40
cornix, cornīcis, *f.,* 32, 35
corvus, corvī, *m.,* 29, 35
gallus, gallī, *m.,* 57
Iūnō, Iūnōnis, *f.,* 49
Iuppiter, Iovis, *m.,* 11
lituus, lituī, *m.,* 8
mīles, mīlitis, *m.,* 13

Minerva, Minervae, *f.,* 40
nūbēs, nūbis, *f.,* 4
oculus, oculī, *m.,* 6, 38
pāvō, pāvōnis, *m.,* 45, 49
penna, pennae, *f.,* 7, 44
    penna alba, 53
    pennae caeruleae, 44
    pennae fuscae, 14
    pennae viridēs, 44
pullus, pullī, *m.,* 54
rōstrum, rōstrī, *n.,* 6
    rōstrum magnum, 21
serpēns, serpentis, *m./f.,* 16
signum, signī, *n.,* 12
vulpēs, vulpis, *f.,* 26
vultur, vulturis, *m.,* 18, 26

Image Credits

Mummy Shroud with Painted Portrait of a Boy (Digital image courtesy of the Getty's Open Content Program)	3
European Cranes (© Estelle R/Shutterstock.com)	4
Eurasian Eagle Owl (© Vaclav Sebek/Shutterstock.com)	6
Owl's Wing Feather (© Gallinago_media/Shutterstock.com)	7
Romulus Receiving the Augury (Open Access image/The Metropolitan Museum of Art)	8
Denarius, issued by Gaius Cassius Longinus and Lentulus Spinther in 42 BCE (© Creative Commons Attribution-Share Alike 3.0 Unported/Classical Numismatic Group, Inc.)	9
Golden Eagle (© Michal Ninger/Shutterstock.com)	10
Jupiter Astride an Eagle, sardonyx cameo fragment (Open Access image/The Metropolitan Museum of Art)	11
Ornament with Eagle (Open Access image/The Cleveland Museum of Art)	12
Roman Standard Bearer (© Lakeview Images/Shutterstock.com)	13
Golden Eagle with Open Beak (© Michal Ninger/Shutterstock.com)	14

Explore Latin: Avēs

Brown Snake Eagle	16
(© Jonathan Oberholster/Shutterstock.com)	
Eagle and Snake, sixth-century CE Byzantine mosaic	17
(© Zzvet/Shutterstock.com)	
Hooded Vulture	18
(© Eric Isselee/Shutterstock.com)	
Golden Eagle with Wings Spread	18
(© withGod/Shutterstock.com)	
Vulture Amulet, Ptolemaic-era glass amulet	20
(Open Access image/The Metropolitan Museum of Art)	
Turkey Vulture	21
(© IN Dancing Light/Shutterstock.com)	
A Flock of Turkey Vultures	22
(© Eric Buermeyer/Shutterstock.com)	
Cinereous Vulture	24
(© Miraleks/Shutterstock.com)	
Birds on a Dead Fox, thirteenth-century CE Franco-Flemish manuscript	26
(Digital image courtesy of the Getty's Open Content Program)	
Common Raven	28
(© Don Mammoser/Shutterstock.com)	
Apollo with a Black Bird, Attic white-ground kylix from a Delphic tomb	29
(© Creative Commons Attribution-Share Alike 2.0/Bibi Saint-Pol)	
Raven with Open Beak	31
(© Grezova Olga/Shutterstock.com)	
The Crow King Consults His Ministers, folio from *Kalila wa Dimna*	33
(Open Access image/The Metropolitan Museum of Art)	
Raven	35
(© Rosa Jay/Shutterstock.com)	
Crow	35
(© Gallinago_media/Shutterstock.com)	

Image Credits

Hooded Crow (© Vishnevskiy Vasily/Shutterstock.com)	37
Terracotta *Lekythos* with an Owl, fourth-century BCE Apulian oil flask (Open Access image/The Metropolitan Museum of Art)	38
Bronze Statuette of Athena Flying Her Owl (Open Access image/The Metropolitan Museum of Art)	40
Athenian Tetradrachm, featuring Athena's owl on the reverse (Open Access image/The Cleveland Museum of Art)	41
Armed Owl, Attic red-figure *oinochoe* in the Louvre Museum (© Creative Commons Attribution-Generic 2.0/Marie-Lan Nguyen)	42
Burrowing Owl (© moosehenderson/Shutterstock.com)	43
Male Peacock (© cynoclub/Shutterstock.com)	44
Peacock Feather (© pixelklex/Shutterstock.com)	44
Mosaic with a Peacock and Flowers, third- or fourth-century CE Byzantine mosaic (Open Access image/The Metropolitan Museum of Art)	45
Wall Fragment with a Peacock (Digital image courtesy of the Getty's Open Content Program)	47
Juno with Peacock, etching by Wenceslaus Hollar (1607–1677) (© Creative Commons Attribution 4.0 International/Wellcome Images)	49
Grave *Naiskos* of a Young Woman, fourth-century BCE Attic grave marker (Digital image courtesy of the Getty's Open Content Program)	50
Mirror with Winged Female Holding Wreath and Goose (Open Access image/The Walters Art Museum)	51

Explore Latin: Avēs

The Geese of the Capitol by Henri-Paul Motte
(1846–1922)   52
(Public Domain)

White Domestic Goose   53
(© DenisNata/Shutterstock.com)

White Feather   53
(© Ilina93/Shutterstock.com)

Walking Chickens   54
(© Hassan Rafi/Unsplash.com)

Bound Rooster, second-century CE Roman mosaic panel
in the Art Institute of Chicago   55
(© Amelia Wallace)

Brown Hen   56
(© Olhastock/Shutterstock.com)

Belly-Amphora (Storage Jar), fifth-century BCE Athenian
black-figure jar   57
(Open Access image/Art Institute of Chicago)

Black Crow over Monuments of Rome   58
(© Juan Garcia Hinojosa/Shutterstock.com)